MARY SEACOLE

Bound *for the* Battlefield

Susan Goldman Rubin

illustrated by **Richie Pope**

CANDLEWICK PRESS

As a child in Kingston, Jamaica, Mary Jane Grant watched her mother pick out a bottle of medicine for a sick British soldier. She always chose the right one. Her mother had made all the medicines herself from flowers and plants. Mary wanted to be a "doctress" just like her mother when she grew up.

Mary pretended that her dolls had the same sicknesses as the soldiers and played at healing them. She was delighted when her dolls' "glow of health" returned. Confidently she extended her practice to dogs and cats around their boardinghouse. But when she forced remedies down the animals' throats and tried to bandage them, they ran away. Soon Mary decided she needed a human patient and might have considered using her younger brother, Edward, and baby sister, Louisa. But she wound up practicing on herself.

She learned from her mother what herbs to use, where to find them, how to prepare them. Mary even tasted them to see how they affected her. "The ambition to become a doctress early took firm root in my mind," she wrote. By the time she was twelve, she was skillful enough to help her mother dress wounds and mix medicines.

At the time Mary was born, in 1805, slavery was practiced in Jamaica. Mary's mother was Creole, meaning she was a descendant of both Europeans and Africans. Because one of her parents was white, she belonged to the class known as free colored. Mary considered herself Creole, too.

She was always proud of her skin color.

Mary's father, James Grant, was a Scottish officer. When Mary was growing up, she loved listening to her father's stories about Scotland's clans and famous battles and his own adventures in the army. He died when Mary was ten. But from him she inherited an urge to travel, which she never lost.

* * *

The Grants owned a boardinghouse, Blundell Hall, near the wharf in the busy port of Kingston, the largest town in Jamaica. Mary stood outside gazing at the tall masts and dreamed of someday sailing to England.

Then, when she was a teenager, some Creole friends unexpectedly invited her to go to London with them. Crossing the Atlantic took eight weeks. The voyage was extremely dangerous, and many passengers got seasick. Not Mary. She enjoyed the voyage, and she loved London. However, one day, when she was out walking arm in arm with her girlfriend from Kingston, some boys on the street jeered at the girls and insulted them about their skin color. This was Mary's first taste of prejudice.

After returning to Kingston, she missed London. She went back when she was eighteen and stayed for two years. When she finally came home, her mother needed her help. An outbreak of yellow fever had hit Jamaica. Soldiers and their families suffered from high fevers, nausea, and violent headaches. Their skin turned pale yellow. Mary and her mother treated the patients with calomel, or mercurous chloride, a salt widely used as a medicine in those days, as well as plantain juice and ginger tea. Mary tenderly nursed the patients while they recovered. She cooked up nourishing broths and stews to help them get strong. When British doctors came to Blundell Hall for a meal, Mary eagerly asked questions. "I had from early youth a yearning for medical knowledge," she wrote.

One of the patients was an Englishman named Edwin Horatio Hamilton Seacole. He shyly kept proposing marriage to her until she said yes. They were married on November 10, 1836, when Mary was thirty-one. From then on Mary was known as Mrs. Mary Seacole. Edwin had relatives in Black River, another busy port in Jamaica. The newlyweds moved there to open a store. But Edwin "was very delicate," wrote Mary. He became so sick that she took him back to Kingston. "I kept him alive by kind nursing and attention as long as I could," she wrote. Sadly he died in October 1844.

Shortly after her husband's death, Mary's mother died, too. Heartbroken, Mary took charge of Blundell

Hall, and her sister, Louisa, helped her. In 1850, an epidemic of cholera swept through Jamaica. In those days, no one understood what caused diseases like cholera. Some doctors believed that people caught it from mysterious "vapours" floating in the air. Soldiers staggered in, complaining of severe diarrhea and vomiting. Their cold skin looked bluish, and many died within hours. Mary suspected that the disease was transmitted from one person to another, an idea that was later proved to be right. She treated patients with her mother's remedies: cinnamon water, fluids mixed with sugar and salt, and mustard plasters applied to the stomach to stimulate circulation.

After the epidemic, Mary decided to visit her brother, Edward, in Cruces, Panama. He had opened a hotel to serve travelers on their way to the gold rush in California. Armed with homemade jam and her medicine chest stocked full of herbal remedies, Mary set out.

No sooner had she arrived than a friend of Edward's became ill after dining at the hotel and died. People accused Edward of poisoning the man. Mary viewed the corpse and recognized signs of cholera: legs doubled up, sunken eyes, and bluish wrinkled skin. The next morning, one of the dead man's friends came down with the familiar symptoms of violent diarrhea and vomiting. There was no doctor in town, only "a little timid dentist." So Mary whipped out her medicine chest and went to work. She applied mustard plasters to the sick man's stomach and back and gave him small doses of calomel, as well as water boiled with cinnamon. "The simplest remedies were perhaps the best," she wrote. Gradually the man recovered, and Mary boasted, "I succeeded in saving my first cholera patient in Cruces."

Cholera spread rapidly, though. During the next few months, Mary took care of many patients, who dubbed her Aunty Seacole. Before leaving Cruces, she attended a Fourth of July party hosted by Americans at her brother's hotel. One of the men offered a toast thanking her for her care. Then he commented that she was a "yaller woman" and that he wished she were "wholly white" so that she would be more "acceptable." The racial slurs angered Mary. Holding her temper, she made a toast hoping that Americans would improve their manners.

Toward the end of 1852, when the rains began, Mary left for Kingston. Once again she suffered an insult because of her race. She boarded an American steamer and seated herself in the lounge. But some American women surrounded her and asked how dare she, as a woman of color, travel with them. Stunned, Mary said she had paid her fare like everyone else. The women uttered bigoted remarks and refused to sit with her. Finally a stewardess was called and told Mary she had to leave. Mary appealed to the stewardess to let her stay on board and said she would sit anywhere, even in a storeroom. But the stewardess said Mary had to get off the boat. Mary was put ashore and had to wait for an English steamer. From then on, she disliked Americans.

She arrived in Kingston just in time for another outbreak of yellow fever. Mary and her sister turned their boardinghouse into a hospital for officers and their families. Following her mother's recipes, Mary faithfully nursed her patients. She wasn't always successful, but she was dedicated. When a young doctor she especially liked lay dying, she stayed at his side as he dictated his will. He left his dog to one friend, his books to another. At the last moment, he asked Mary to hold him in her arms like a mother. "Home! Home!" he cried. She wept as he passed away. A few months later, Mary received a letter from his mother thanking her for her kindness. Enclosed was a gold pin with a twist of the young man's hair as a remembrance.

At that time, the Crimean War between Russia and Turkey had begun. Czar Nicholas I of Russia had sent troops to occupy Crimea, a Turkish peninsula in the Black Sea. He wanted to both expand Russia's territory and control churches in the Middle East. The czar thought that Britain and Austria would support him. But the British people were furious. In March 1854, Britain and France entered the war as allies of the Turks. Mary read newspaper reports that more men were dying from disease than from bullets. There weren't enough doctors and nurses to care for the soldiers.

"I made up my mind," she wrote, "that if the army wanted nurses, they would be glad of me. . . . I decided that I *would* go to the Crimea." She sailed to England

and went straight to London. Decked out in her favorite yellow dress and blue bonnet trimmed with red ribbons, she marched into the War Office and volunteered as an army nurse. The authorities laughed at her.

Nursing was a new profession then, only just becoming a respectable career for women. The most famous nurse of the time was Florence Nightingale. The War Department had asked her to lead a team of thirty-eight nurses to the Crimea. More would be needed. So Mary applied for the job. Nightingale was already in Crimea, but the interviewer told Mary that the positions had been filled. And when Mary reapplied, she was turned down again. Mary could tell that they didn't want her because she was a "yellow woman." It seemed that the English were as prejudiced toward her "duskier skin" as Americans were.

"Tears streamed down my foolish cheeks," she wrote.

But the next day, she perked up and hatched a plan. She would open her own convalescent home in the Crimea to nurse invalids. Mary had years of experience. A relative of her husband's, Thomas Day, agreed to be her business partner. Mary spent all her money to stock

up on medicines, bandages, and "home comforts" she thought would come in handy. In January 1855, at the age of fifty, she sailed for Constantinople, in Turkey.

Upon arriving, she went to visit Florence Nightingale at the army hospital, across the river in Scutari. When Mary entered the hospital, she was appalled. The place stank! It was built over an open sewer. There was no fresh air, and there were not enough beds.

Nightingale had been horrified, too, when she had first set foot there. Old sewer pipes beneath the building had burst. Toilets overflowed, and the floors were covered with filth. More soldiers were sick due to unsanitary conditions than any other cause. Nightingale had tried to make improvements such as washing down the walls with lime and providing clean bedding for the men.

An officer Mary had treated in Kingston recognized her and escorted her through the halls. "Wards of sufferers, lying there so quiet and still" brought tears to her eyes. A patient with "a shaven bandaged head" called out, "Mother Seacole! Mother Seacole!" and she sat at his bedside, cheering him up. As Mary walked through the "miles of suffering in that great hospital," she couldn't resist "replacing a slipped bandage" or loosening one that was too tight.

Finally she went to the nurses' quarters to pay her respects to the famous "Lady with the Lamp." When they were introduced, Nightingale said, "What do you want, Mrs. Seacole—anything that we can do for you?" By now it was late and Mary needed a place to sleep. She offered to "nurse the sick for the night" in exchange for a bed. Nightingale refused her services. Her staff of professionals had trained in hospitals and convents. Besides, the building was already overcrowded. Fourteen nurses shared one room, and ten nuns were in another. So she sent Mary down to the washerwomen's quarters. Later Nightingale wrote in a letter, "I had the greatest difficulty in repelling Mrs. Seacole's advances, & in preventing association between her and my nurses (absolutely out of the question). . . . But I was successful."

Nightingale considered Mary totally unfit as a nurse because she came from a different class in society, had dark skin, and was a "woman of bad character," occasionally giving sickly soldiers a swig of sherry or a sip of a claret cup, a kind of wine lemonade.

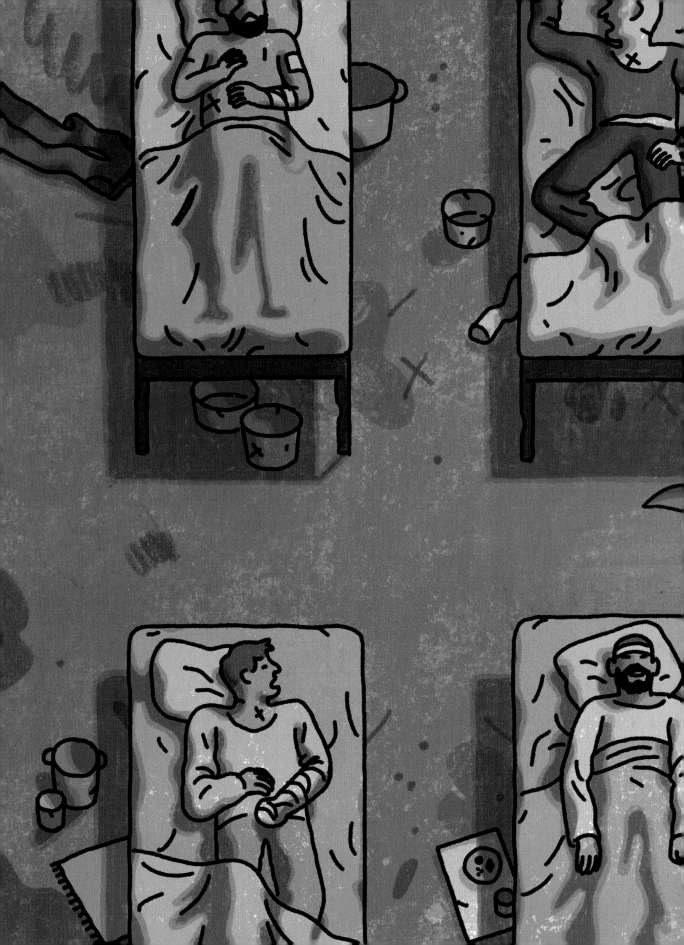

In the morning, Mary left for Balaclava, near the battlefield. "I had plenty of difficulties to contend with," she wrote. The work was hard, and thieves stole her supplies. First she supervised the unloading of her supplies and stacked them on the beach, covering them with tarpaulin. At night she had to stay on an ammunitions ship. Climbing up the ladder to board the ship was not easy for a "plump person," as she described herself, and more than once she almost fell into the harbor.

During the night, French Zouave soldiers stole her goods. "Of course we hired men to watch," said Mary, but the watchmen either ignored the robbers or stole things, too. So Mary had to hire new guards and send for more stuff.

Every day on the beach, she helped the doctors transfer sick and wounded soldiers to ships bound for Florence Nightingale's hospital in Scutari. In the cold rain, Mary set up a stove and kettle and brewed tea. She brought mugs to the men, who were grateful for "the warm and comforting beverage." They named her

"Creole with the tea mug." She gently held their hands, whispered something about hope, and often listened to their dying words.

One day she heard a sailor shout, "Why, as I live, if this ain't Aunty Seacole, of Jamaica! Shiver all that's left of my poor timbers." It was a sailor she had treated back in Kingston. He had lost his leg fighting the Russians. Mary said, "I'm sorry to see you in this sad plight."

He said, "Never fear for me, Aunty Seacole; I'll make the best of the leg the Rooshians [Russians] have left me." She gave him lemonade and some sponge cake that she had made because "it tasted of 'home,'" and soon he was joking with his mates.

When the weather grew milder, Mary and her partner, Thomas Day, chose a place for their building. She named the spot Spring Hill, and construction of the British Hotel began, using driftwood, shipping crates, and any pieces of iron sheeting she could find. "Everything, although rough and unpolished, was comfortable and warm," she wrote.

British officers flocked to the hotel for nourishing food like they ate at home.

Mary boasted, "If I had nothing else to be proud of, I think my rice-puddings, made without milk . . . would have gained me a reputation." She said, "Whenever I had a few leisure moments, I used to wash my hands, roll up my sleeves and roll out pastry."

She and Day had to replenish their stock of supplies. So they charged those who could afford it for meals. When soldiers had no money, Mary simply gave them food or said they could pay her later.

The men called her Mother Seacole, and she thought of them as her sons. The color of her skin didn't matter to them, and they treated her with respect as well as affection, unlike bigots she had known. Sometimes the sick soldiers in huts and trenches sent for something to eat. On horseback, Mary delivered a "cooling drink, a little broth, some homely cake."

"I was frequently 'under fire,'" she wrote. "One could scarcely move about the various camps without some risk." As she made her rounds, Russian bullets and shells whizzed overhead. Soldiers shouted, "Lie down,

mother, lie down!" and she had to dive to the ground for cover. Once she fell so hard that she dislocated her thumb.

During a lull in the fighting, officers came to the British Hotel for medical treatment. It was like a convalescent hospital. Mary took care of all kinds of problems, from frostbitten fingers and feet to dysentery and diarrhea. She ladled out remedies that she mixed in a large pan, and grateful patients later wrote thank-you notes.

Meanwhile Florence Nightingale had arrived to inspect the Balaclava hospitals nearby. She collapsed and became sick with "Crimean fever," a form of typhus. Mary promised to visit her and "sort the 'dear lady' out with some treatment."

Nightingale was revolted by the idea and discouraged Mary from coming to "quack" her with Creole medicines. She sneered at Mary's herbal cures and regarded her as a phony because of her skin color and background.

At that time, tourists visited the Crimea like sightseers to view the battles. It was a common though ghoulish activity. Many travelers stayed at the British Hotel and watched the fighting from a safe spot on Cathcart's Hill. Mary, recalling her father's stories, witnessed the allies advancing toward the Russians. "This was my first experience of actual battle," she wrote.

In June, Mary busily prepared cheese sandwiches to serve as refreshments for the spectators and officers, packed her large bag full of bandages, needles, thread, and medicine, and set off for battle. Wearing pearls, earrings, and a brilliant blue dress, she slung her bag over her shoulder and rode up to Cathcart's Hill. When the fighting started, Mary got a pass to go down and help the doctors hard at work. "Upon the way . . . I was 'under fire,'" she wrote. "A shot would come ploughing up the ground and raising clouds of dust." But the words of appreciation she received made it worth risking her life.

Mary was so busy during the battle that she didn't know who was winning until she returned to the hotel. The news was bad. The allies were losing. Two of the British leaders she had known were killed. The next day, Mary rushed back to the scene. "That battle-field was a fearful sight for a woman to witness," she wrote. The following week, another great British general died. Mary attended the funeral and wrote, "The guns thundered forth in sorrow, not in anger."

Summer heat brought a new menace: flies. "There was no escaping from them by night or by day," wrote Mary. One of her "customers," Prince Viktor, a nephew of Queen Victoria, came to Mary for help. His face was covered with insect bites. "Mami," he said, calling her by the name used by Creole children in the West Indies, where he had served, "these flies respect nothing. . . . They'll kill me, mami; they're everywhere, even in the trenches. . . . What can you do for me, mami?"

She bought a piece of muslin and quickly pinned up a makeshift mosquito net for the prince. He was delighted and never forgot her good deed.

By late summer, rumors spread that another big battle was about to be fought. At dawn on August 16, Mary heard heavy firing. She took off with her medicine bag and baskets of supplies. From her perch on Cathcart's Hill, she saw the Russian soldiers cross the Tchernaya River. The English and French cavalry drew up for a surprise attack. They stormed the Russians and forced them back.

When the fighting seemed to have stopped, Mary hurried down to the field and attended to the wounded. She "helped to lift them into the ambulances, which came tearing up to the scene of action." She even assisted some Russians. One of them, a handsome officer who had been shot in the side, took a ring off his finger and gave it to her. He kissed her hand and smiled in gratitude. That day, Mary received many thanks, she said, "in that one common language of the whole world—smiles."

She personally carried two patients off the field. One was a French officer she took back to the British Hotel for treatment. The other was a Russian colt. "The colt was already wounded in the ears and fore-foot," wrote Mary. A French corporal was about to shoot the animal because of its injuries. But Mary paid him to bring the colt to the hotel. Mary nursed the horse the way she had taken care of animals when she was a child. The colt became her pet, and she later arranged to have it sail back to England with her.

* * *

In the following weeks, there was a continuous roar of gunfire. The allies bombarded Sebastopol, the Russian stronghold. One night Mary stayed up to see the spectacle of Sebastopol burning. Ships blazed in the harbor. On the morning of September 8, she had a tip from officers that another battle was about to start. Mary set out on horseback, ready to help.

Sentries would not allow anyone to go up to Cathcart's Hill. But when they realized who Mary was, they let her pass. By noon, the French Zouaves had captured a tower held by the Russians. Then, in horror, Mary watched thousands of British troops surge forward, only to be shot down. Their attack had failed.

There were more wounded for her to take care of than at the last battle. Worst of all, she recognized officers she had treated back in Kingston. "Their loss was terrible," she wrote. Meanwhile the Russians kept firing shells. "One fell so near," she recalled, "that I thought my last hour was come." She threw herself on the ground and was so frightened that she remained there until she heard laughter from those around her. Realizing that the danger had passed, she stood up, dusted herself off, and took a piece of the shell as a souvenir.

All along, a journalist had been noticing her. And she had spotted him sketching and taking notes for his newspaper. His name was William Russell, and he was the first war correspondent. Mary praised him for "finding time, even in his busiest moment, to lend a helping hand to the wounded." And Russell applauded her efforts in the London *Times.* Unbeknownst to Mary, she was becoming famous in England because of Russell's stories about her.

By September 9, the allies had conquered Sebastopol and the Russians had retreated. Mary knew the men would be famished after days of fighting, so she brought food. "Explosions were taking place in all directions," she recalled. "Every step had a score of dangers." Yet she fearlessly made her deliveries.

With news of the allied victory, tourists thronged Sebastopol. Some of them took pictures with a new invention, the camera. The allies celebrated with picnics, dinner parties, and cricket matches.

By New Year's, said Mary, "we all began to think of going home."

Peace negotiations opened in Paris in February 1856, and on March 30, an armistice treaty was signed. The war was over.

Before leaving the Crimea, Mary visited the cemeteries "where friends rested so calmly." She planted "shrubs and flowers, little lilac trees . . . and flowering evergreens." And from many graves she picked wildflowers and tufts of grass to bring home to relatives as remembrances of their loved ones.

At the end of June, Mary sailed back to England. "I returned bankrupt," she wrote. "I found myself poor." She faced piles of unpaid bills. Many soldiers who had promised to pay her back for her services never did. But the reporter William Russell and other good friends established a fund to help her. Contributions trickled in.

Meanwhile a publisher asked Mary to write an eyewitness account of the Crimean War. So she began her autobiography, *Wonderful Adventures of Mrs. Seacole in Many Lands.* Russell wrote the introduction. The book was

published in July 1857, and the cover featured a portrait of Mary with her bonnet and medicine bag. A benefit concert to promote the book was held at the Royal Surrey Gardens. At the end, thousands of people in the audience shouted Mary's name and cheered her.

In 1860, she moved back to Kingston and stayed with her sister, who still ran the boardinghouse. In London, another fund was set up to aid Mary. This time it was headed by Prince Viktor, the officer she had treated for insect bites. The prince, later known as Count Gleichen, asked his aunt, Queen Victoria, to chip in. It is believed that Queen Victoria finally made a donation, too.

Now Mary was able to pay off her debts and buy a bungalow in Kingston. But when the Franco-Prussian War broke out, in 1870, she read that men and women with "surgical knowledge" were needed to nurse the wounded. So at age sixty-five, she volunteered immediately. Once again she was bound for the battlefield. However, officials wouldn't let her go because she was "'too precious' to lose."

* * *

Mary moved back to London and was living there when she died, on May 14, 1881. She was seventy-six. Her dear friend Count Gleichen had become an artist and had sculpted a bust of her wearing pearls, earrings, and three medals. He titled his sculpture "Mary Seacole, the Celebrated Crimean Heroine."

In her will, Mary left most of her belongings to her sister, nieces, nephews, and cousins. But to Count Gleichen's daughter she left her "best set of pearl ornaments."

The count's sculpture of Mary Seacole now rests on a pedestal at the Institute of Jamaica. And a portrait of her in earrings and medals (no pearls) by Albert Charles Challen hangs in the National Portrait Gallery in London. Nursing schools, streets, and roads throughout Britain and Jamaica have been named for her. To this day, the adventurous Mary Seacole is lovingly honored and remembered.

Source Notes

p. 1: "glow of health": Seacole, p. 12.

p. 1: extended her practice: ibid.

p. 2: "The ambition . . . in my mind": ibid.

p. 6: "I had from . . . medical knowledge": ibid.

p. 6: "was very delicate" and "I kept him alive . . . as I could": ibid., p. 14.

p. 7: "vapours": McDonald, p. 101.

p. 8: "a little timid dentist": Seacole, p. 30.

p. 8: "The simplest remedies . . . the best": ibid., p. 34.

p. 8: "I succeeded . . . in Cruces": ibid., p. 30.

p. 8: "yaller woman," "wholly white," and "acceptable": ibid., p. 49.

p. 12: "Home! Home!" ibid., p. 61.

p. 12: "I made up . . . to the Crimea": ibid., p. 71.

p. 14: "yellow woman": ibid., p. 73.

p. 14: "duskier skin" and "tears streamed . . . foolish cheeks": ibid., p. 74.

p. 17: "home comforts": ibid., p. 75.

p. 17: "Wards of . . . quiet and still": ibid., p. 79.

p. 17: "a shaven bandaged head": ibid., p. 80.

p. 17: "Mother Seacole! Mother Seacole!": ibid., p. 80

p. 17: "miles of suffering . . . hospital": ibid.

p. 18: "replacing a slipped bandage": ibid.

p. 18: "Lady with the Lamp": Robinson, p. 122; McDonald, p. 71.

p. 18: "What do you want . . . do for you?": quoted in Seacole, p. 82.

p. 18: "nurse the sick for the night": ibid.

p. 18: "I had the greatest . . . was successful": quoted in Robinson, p. 191.

p. 18: "woman of bad character": ibid., p. 123.

p. 22: "I had plenty . . . contend with": Seacole, p. 86.

p. 22: "plump person": ibid., p. 83.

p. 22: "Of course we hired men to watch": ibid., p. 93.

p. 22: "the warm and comforting beverage": Robinson, p. 107.

p. 23: "Creole with the tea mug": ibid., p. 117.

p. 23: "Why, as I live . . . poor timbers": quoted in Seacole, p. 90.

p. 23: "I'm sorry to . . . sad plight": ibid.

p. 23: "Never fear . . . have left me": ibid.

p. 23: "it tasted of 'home'": ibid., p. 91.

p. 23: "Everything, although rough . . . and warm": ibid., p. 102.

p. 24: "If I had nothing . . . me a reputation": ibid., p. 123.

p. 24: "Whenever I had . . . roll out pastry": ibid.

p. 24: "cooling drink . . . homely cake": ibid., p. 111.

p. 24: "I was frequently 'under fire'": ibid., p. 134.

p. 24: "One could scarcely . . . without some risk": ibid.

pp. 24, 27: "Lie down . . . lie down!": ibid., p. 136.

p. 27: "Crimean fever": ibid., p. 129.

p. 27: "sort the 'dear . . . some treatment": Robinson, p. 119.

p. 27: "quack": ibid., p. 123.

p. 28: "This was my . . . actual battle": Seacole, p. 129.

p. 28: "Upon the way . . . 'under fire'": ibid., p. 136.

p. 28: "A shot would . . . clouds of dust": ibid.

p. 28: "That battle-field was . . . woman to witness": ibid., p. 138.

p. 29: "The guns thundered . . . not in anger": ibid., p. 139.

p. 29: "There was no . . . or by day": ibid., p. 140.

p. 29: "customers": ibid.

p. 29: "Mami, these flies . . . do for me, mami?": ibid., p. 141.

p. 30: "helped to . . . scene of action": ibid., p. 142.

p. 30: "in that one common . . . smiles": ibid., p. 143.

p. 30: "The colt was . . . and fore-foot": ibid.

p. 33: "Their loss was terrible": ibid., p. 147.

p. 33: "One fell so near . . . hour was come": ibid.

p. 34: "finding time . . . to the wounded": ibid., p. 148.

p. 34: "Explosions were . . . score of dangers": ibid., p. 149.

p. 35: "We all began . . . going home": ibid., p. 161.

p. 35: "where friends rested so calmly": ibid., p. 166.

p. 35: "shrubs and flowers . . . flowering evergreens": ibid.

p. 35: "I returned bankrupt" and "I found myself poor": ibid., p. 170.

p. 37: "surgical knowledge": Robinson, p. 189.

p. 37: "'too precious' to lose": ibid., p. 192.

p. 38: "Mary Seacole . . . Crimean Heroine": ibid., p. 214.

p. 38: "best set of pearl ornaments": ibid., p. 196.

Bibliography

McDonald, Lynn. *Florence Nightingale at First Hand.* London: Continuum, 2010.

Robinson, Jane. *Mary Seacole: The Most Famous Black Woman of the Victorian Age.* New York: Carroll & Graf, 2004.

Seacole, Mary. *Wonderful Adventures of Mrs. Seacole in Many Lands.* Edited by Sara Salih. London: Penguin, 2005. First published 1857 by James Blackwell (London).

For John Harris

SGR

To my mother, Rosemarie McCoy,
a registered nurse

RP

·⋘⋙·

First edition 2020

Library of Congress Catalog Card Number pending
ISBN 978-0-7636-7994-1

20 21 22 23 24 25 LEO 10 9 8 7 6 5 4 3 2 1

Printed in Heshan, Guangdong, China

This book was typeset in Mrs Eaves and Charcuterie.
The illustrations were created digitally.

Candlewick Press
99 Dover Street
Somerville, Massachusetts 02144

www.candlewick.com